Dr. Chico D. Stars

Root Cal Specialist
to the
STARS!

5/13/11

"You are in for a real treat. Dr. Rico Short has authored a literary master piece, a wealth of information, wit and wisdom that will change your life if you let it."

Dr. Leonard Scott, DDS
Pastor, Rock Community Church
President, Tyscot Records

"WOW! What an incredible journey you must have been on to have compiled some of the most practical & powerful truths assembled in a single book!"

Dr. Jim Bolin,
Bishop, Trinity Chapel
Powder Springs, GA

"Dr. Rico Short is a refreshingly authentic leader who has the unique ability to communicate in both a challenging and encouraging style."

Jason Bolin
Senior Pastor, Trinity Chapel

"In "Getting to the Root of your Problem" Dr. Short does even more than that, extracting nuggets of inspiration and affirmation for your daily healing and prosperity."

Fonzworth Bentley
Musician & Author
"Advance Your Swagger: How to Use Manners, Confidence, and Style to Get Ahead"

Getting to the Root of your Problem
365 Days of Inspirational Thinking

Dr. Rico D. Short

authorHOUSE®

AuthorHouse™
1663 Liberty Drive
Bloomington, IN 47403
www.authorhouse.com
Phone: 1-800-839-8640

© 2011 Dr. Rico D. Short. All rights reserved.

No part of this book may be reproduced, stored in a retrieval system, or transmitted by any means without the written permission of the author.

First published by AuthorHouse   3/24/2011

ISBN: 978-1-4567-5245-3 (e)
ISBN: 978-1-4567-5244-6 (dj)
ISBN: 978-1-4567-5241-5 (sc)

Library of Congress Control Number: 2011903726

Printed in the United States of America

Any people depicted in stock imagery provided by Thinkstock are models, and such images are being used for illustrative purposes only. Certain stock imagery © Thinkstock.

This book is printed on acid-free paper.

Because of the dynamic nature of the Internet, any web addresses or links contained in this book may have changed since publication and may no longer be valid. The views expressed in this work are solely those of the author and do not necessarily reflect the views of the publisher, and the publisher hereby disclaims any responsibility for them.

I would like to thank Dr. Leonard Scott and Dr. Jim Bolin for reviewing the accuracy and content of the book.
Dr. Rico D. Short
Board Certified Endodontist
Motivational Speaker
Apex Endodontics P.C.
Smyrna, Georgia 30127
www.apexendodontics.net
dr.short@yahoo.com
Cover and Photos—Patrick Albright
Medialance Design Studio, www.medialancedesign.com
AuthorHouse Publishing

For God, who gave me the vision, courage, and inspiration to put my thoughts in writing and share them with others.
Also for
my Proverbs 31 wife, Angela;
my children, Ava and Jayla;
my mother, Shirva Short; and
my family, friends, pastors, teachers, and mentors.

In special loving memory of my grandmother, Mrs. Carrie "Mudear" Short

Introduction

I am an endodontist (root canal specialist) by profession. Don't worry, this book has nothing to do with root canals, but it does have information on *pain*—how to avoid some pains in life and how pain can influence our lives, good and bad!

I believe that motivational and inspirational words are the keys to a successful life. I have always wanted to write a book about changing lives from a personal perspective, based on my relationship with God. This is it!

I hope this book inspires, gives hope, and ignites dreams to come to reality daily in the hearts and minds of all people. Life is full of change and challenges that we all must face. However, the determining factor is how we allow them to affect our lives.

Let's get to the *ROOT* of your problem!

Day 1

We were all created in the image of God. God took His DNA and implanted it in the spirit of man. Therefore, originally, we were all the same in spirit. The difference came when we were influenced by sin from birth.

Day 2

Did you have a choice of your race, color, or nationality before you were born? No—but God did! You belonging to your family is no accident. Whether rich, poor, or in between, God purposed a plan for you to positively influence others around just you. That's one reason why you did not have a choice!

Day 3

God is love and has no color. That's why true love is colorblind.

Day 4

Have you discovered your God-given gift yet? If not, here are four questions that will help you:
1. What do you enjoy doing or what are you good at?
2. What comes naturally to you?
3. Would you do it even if you did not get paid?
4. Will it make a positive difference in the lives of others?

Day 5

Everyone likes investing in things with an instant return. Have you ever thought about investing in peace? Peace is an investment whose returns are sometimes not seen immediately. Peace does not come automatically. You have to want it and fight to keep it. Not arguing with your spouse can be a good start. Peace is more precious than fortune and fame because without it you can't enjoy either!

Day 6

One of the best tricks Satan uses is to convince people that he really does not exist—except on Halloween!

Day 7

Satan is good at using reverse psychology. He tries to convince godly folks to become close friends with ungodly people. Satan usually whispers that by being friends with ungodly people, you can win them over to God. I am not saying that we should avoid evil people or be unkind to them. However, we can't become too close to those who habitually practice wrongdoing. This has corrupted many godly people.

Day 8

It is amazing to see people who believe in magic, which is an illusion, and not believe in God, who is real!

Day 9

For those of you who enjoy speaking encouraging words, don't get caught up in the number of people who acknowledge your good works. Keep speaking positively anyway! There are people who listen to your words and are encouraged by them, but they don't want anyone else to know that they are on board with you.

Day 10

If Jesus was to post His sermons on Facebook or Twitter back in the day, I don't think many would check "I like his status!"

Day 11

Do you know people who always seem to be anxious or afraid? Perhaps they are spiritually weak. They need to be spiritually trained by the Holy Spirit. The Holy Spirit is the Christian's "muscle" waiting to be flexed, exercised, and employed in every moment of the believer's life. If you are a believer, you have the Holy Spirit (strength of God) in you to change your situation and remove fear. The more you exercise the Holy Spirit in your life, the faster fear is replaced by faith!

Day 12

Why don't people at church praise and worship God the same way that they cheer at their favorite football game? Imagine all the people in the Georgia Dome at a Falcons game on one accord worshipping God in spirit and in truth that place may literally rock! We might be visited by a few confused angels thinking they are in heaven!

Day 13

"And all the people followed Solomon into Jerusalem, playing flutes and shouting for joy. The celebration was so joyous and noisy that the earth shook with the sound" (1 Kings 1:38).

Day 14

Can you think of a time or situation when you could have been killed or could have been in a lot of trouble, but somehow you got out of it? That's God interrupting what was meant to destroy you from your *purpose*. God only preserves what has purpose and meaning!

Day 15

Lord, I thank You for the good friends that You have surrounded me with. Help Your people in all walks of life who are struggling with the threat of unrighteous relationships. Do not allow us to turn our backs on those who need our help and prayers. However, help us to cut all ties with those who would lead us into wickedness. Fill us with Your Spirit today to be more like You. Amen.

Day 16

"Doors will open when you find the missing key." The lyrics in "Thank Me Now," by rapper-singer Drake, were originally in the Bible in Proverbs—by God!

Day 17

Some of you are preserving your cash because of fear of the economy. In the meantime, the interest is killing you! Pay off your debts if you have the money, but make sure that you have some left over for emergencies—at least one month's reserve. Debt is of the devil!

Day 18

Too many people put off going to school because of cost. Investing in yourself is priceless, especially when it comes to education that will pay off later. A student loan is one of the best investment tools you can ever get. Creditors can repossess items bought by other loans, but they can't repossess knowledge gained through education.

Day 19

If anyone is in Christ, he is a new creation; old things have passed away; behold, all things have become new - (2 Corinthians 5:17). However, this is not in our flesh, nor in our soul—just in our Spirit. It is a constant battle, because our minds and bodies have to be renewed by the Word of God daily!

Day 20

Sometimes when reading the Bible online, it may say, "Web Shield Alert! Threat detected Threat name: Exploit Fragus Exploit Kit (type 905)." Satan wants to keep you from the truth! He does not want you to be empowered by the word! More words equal more power!

Day 21

How do I renew my mind?
1. Choose what you think about (guard your heart, because it determines your path).
2. Change your automatic pilot.
3. Go to the root of the problem.
4. Choose to depend on the Holy Spirit.

—Pastor Jason Bolin

Day 22

God says, "My people are destroyed for lack of knowledge," which is in the Word. When you are spiritually ignorant, it's like going to war with a butter knife! Get the Word of God into your heart by reading, listening, and speaking it! God has provided it all in Jesus Christ, but it is up to us to individually get into the Word of God and learn who we are and what we have!

Day 23

God desires for all to be saved! There are no such things as secular church folks! We all belong to Him! "All of us must die eventually. Our lives are like water spilled out on the ground, which cannot be gathered up again. But God does not just sweep life away; instead, he devises ways to bring us back when we have been separated from him" (2 Samuel 14:14).

Day 24

There are some churches so bound in tradition that they receive very little spiritual insight. For example, some groups believe in no instruments in church. Why? They probably do not understanding the spiritual meaning of Ephesians 5:19–20: "Speaking to yourselves in psalms and hymns and spiritual songs, singing and making melody in your heart to the Lord."

This is what the amplified bible says:

Ephesians 5:19–20:

- "Speak out to one another in psalms and hymns and spiritual songs, offering praise with voices [and instruments] and making melody with all your heart to the Lord …"
- Now, did you know when you sing you are actually making music (creating notes and harmony)?
- David sang praises and danced to the Lord until his clothes virtually fell off!
- David actually played the harp to soothe Saul when he was stressed out.
- Lucifer (Satan) was the minister of music in heaven before he sinned and committed high treason against God!

Do you think the angels in heaven, who are made below us, are making music in their "hearts"? No! Their job is to serve and praise out loud!

Day 25

"Do you need wisdom? Ask him who made it all! This is what the Lord says, he who made the earth, the Lord who formed it and established it —the Lord is his name: Call to me and I will answer you and tell you great and unsearchable things you do not know" (Jeremiah 33:2–3, NIV).

Day 26

"The Lord does not look at the things man looks at. Man looks at the outward appearance, but the Lord looks at the heart" (1 Samuel 16:7, NIV).

Day 27

The Holy Spirit breaks through the walls of sin, guilt, and shame because there is now no condemnation for those who are in Christ. The Holy Spirit elevates our view off of earthly things and onto the things of God, spiritual things that are eternal.

Day 28

"The Holy Spirit is described actually like a person. He has a mind, will, and emotions. The Holy Spirit helps, teaches, guides, and comforts, as well as performs other functions. Just like throwing a bucket of water on a fire can quench the fire, you can do the same thing to the Holy Spirit by actions and attitudes that are inconsistent with what the believers as a body are doing."

—Pastor K. C. Price

Day 29

"The Godhead (Trinity) functions like a corporation. God the Father is the president and chief executive officer. Jesus is the executive vice president and director of operations. The Holy Spirit is the field representative. All three are God, but all have different functions."

—Pastor K. C. Price

Day 30

Did you know that one of the greatest tragedies of life is to go to church but never execute the Word? It's like having a key to get out of jail but being too lazy to put it in the lock and push! "Do not merely listen to the word, and so deceive yourselves. Do what it says" (James 1:22, NIV).

Day 31

If you can't sleep, maybe you need to get up and pray! Somebody always needs prayer! The Lord always wants to hear from you. Just one word from God possesses dynamos (the power to change things or to be explosive like dynamite) in your life!

Day 32

According to the Bible, you are not a child of God unless you believe in, rely on, and trust in Jesus! If not, you are just His creation! "To all who received him, to those who believe in his name, he gave the right to become children of God —children born not of natural descent, nor of human decision or a husband's will, but born of God" (John 1:12–13, NIV).

Day 33

As a child of God, there are special privileges—but even more responsibilities.

Day 34

Today, choose to use the things and gifts of the spirit God has blessed you with to draw people not to yourself, but to Christ. Jesus said, "You are the light of the world. Let your light shine before men, that they may see your good deeds and praise your Father in heaven" (Matthew 5:14–16, NIV).

Day 35

Did you know that God has given everyone a life preserver called the Bible? "I will never forget your precepts, for by them, you have *preserved my life*" (Psalms 119:93, NIV).

Day 36

"To win our spiritual battles, we must be aggressive against our enemy, Satan. We cannot be passive. We must take the initiative. Ours must be the offensive position, rather than the defensive. Truly God is calling His people to rise up and war against their enemy. We're in a war—let's go!"
—Bible.com

Day 37

If today has not been a good day for you so far, keep pressing through with a smile on your face and keep your head up high! It will soon be over! "I press on toward the goal to win the prize for which God has called me heavenward in Christ Jesus" (Philippians 3:14, NIV).

Day 38

Today I finished a rather difficult surgery. At the end, the patient said, "That's it?" I said, "Yes!" She did mention that she prayed before the surgery and I prayed before performing the surgery, and God did the rest! The next time you need surgery, please pray and don't be offended to ask the doctor to pray as well before the surgery!

Day 39

Are you tired of going to a stiff church? No music or depressing music at best just dead! Well, you don't have to tolerate that! You can really act like a fool when worshiping God oh yeah like David did! "I was dancing before the Lord so I celebrate before the Lord. Yes, and I am willing to look even more foolish than this, even to be humiliated in my own eyes!" (2 Samuel 6:21).

Day 40

When I say "Let's go!" it's like saying *Amen* (which means so be it and to be in agreement with). Let's go together!

Day 41

The Christ-like life is a marathon—not a sprint! To persevere means to be persistent and refuse to stop: asking, seeking, knocking, praying, working, loving, helping, and giving to God and others. God honors that and He will honor you in due season. When is due season coming? When it comes! "Let us run with perseverance the race marked out for us" (Hebrews 12:1).

Day 42

You see, things are not always what they seem! Be careful trying to be like the Joneses and be like Jesus!

Day 43
God wants to do big things in your life! Do you know what one of my secrets to success is? Faith! (I saw, spoke, and worked myself into this position.) Now what is faith? "Faith is being sure of what we hope for and certain of what we do not see" (Hebrews 11:1, NIV). There was a time when I did not see how it was going to work out, but I believed anyway! Where is your faith now?

Day 44
Do you want to be a famous rock star, rapper, or R & B singer? That's cool, but more importantly, God wants you to be a star for the rock (Christ, that is). The ice, the car, the house, the clothes should be used to give God glory! He is exquisitely eloquently divine!

Day 45

Pray this prayer today: Lord, thank you for all the wonderful things You have given me to enjoy in this life. However, I never want to be guilty of allowing those things that bring pleasure to become more important than the things of God. May I always put You and Your will first in my life. Today give me the strength and encouragement to stand for righteousness despite my sins. In Jesus's name, amen!

Day 46

Endurance! Life is not a sprint, but more like a marathon! We may fall down, but we will get back up. This is our heritage and lifestyle as a Christian! The race does not always go to the fastest, but to those who endure to the end! Don't give up!

Day 47

Today I was able to bless a man I hardly knew and his family. Their house was foreclosed on. What a better world it would be if more people did this! We are blessed to be a blessing! Who have you helped lately?

Day 48

Do you want good to come to you? Then you must give and run your business with honesty and integrity! "Good will come to him who is generous and lends freely, who conducts his affairs with justice" (Psalms 112:5, NIV).

Day 49

Some of you are not getting your prayers answered because you are relying on someone else's faith and prayers (e.g., mom, dad, grandmother, pastor). Jesus asked, "What about you? Who do you say that I am?" Simon Peter answered, "You are the Christ, the Son of the living God" (Matthew 16:15–16, NIV). You need to develop a personal relationship with Christ. Start where you are right now. You don't have to clean yourself up first!

Day 50

People may call you "Doctor," but are you board-certified? They may call you "Attorney," but have you passed the bar? They may call you "Pastor," but is there anything about your life that would testify to the fact that you're anything other than a pastor? It's not the title, it's the testimony. Let your life speak about your title!

Day 51

Today, actively look for ways to serve God and serve others. Go out of your way to serve someone and don't just do it to do it. Let that person know you're helping them out because your service pleases the Lord you love! "Therefore, my dear brothers, stand firm. Let nothing move you. Always give yourselves fully to the work of the Lord, because you know that your labor in the Lord is not in vain" (1 Corinthians 15:58).

Day 52

Do you want to know how to get purified of all your sins no matter how bad? "If we walk in the light, as he is in the light, we have fellowship with one another, and the blood of Jesus, his Son, purifies us from all sin" (1 John 1:7, NIV). It's purified not by what you do, but by what Jesus's blood did!

Day 53

If you go against God's grain, expect some splinters.
—Author unknown

Day 54

To fear means to not have faith. Without faith, you can't please God. You only need a little to start with like a mustard seed. Faith is of God and fear is of the devil! The Lord says, "Do not fear, for I am with you; do not be dismayed, for I am your God. I will strengthen you and help you; I will uphold you with my righteous right hand" (Isaiah 41:10, NIV).

Day 55

Then I heard a strong voice out of Heaven saying, "Salvation and power are established! Kingdom of our God, authority of his Messiah! The accuser of our brothers and sisters is thrown out, who accused them day and night before God. They defeated him through the blood of the Lamb and the bold word of their witness" (Revelation 12:10–11, MSG).

Day 56

Did you know that Satan accuses you of not being worthy of God's love when you sin (miss the mark)? He presents himself to God and in your mind to wreak havoc. One way to defeat this attack is by pleading the blood of Jesus over whatever situation comes against you. In addition, your testimony (something in which God supernaturally brought you through) brings more power to the situation and ultimately diffuses it. That's the combo punch that every Christian needs in order to be victorious in this life!

Day 57

How do you feel about talking to someone about Jesus? Afraid, embarrassed, ashamed, or that it's unimportant? You may be the only link for that person to inherit eternal life! "I am not ashamed of the gospel, because it is the power of God for the salvation of everyone who believes" (Romans 1:16, NIV).

Day 58

You can do all things through Christ and can win no matter the outcome! "In Christ, all the fullness of the Deity lives in bodily form, and you have been given fullness in Christ, who is the head over every power and authority" (Colossians 2:9–10, NIV).

Day 59

Do you need a life facelift? "Get rid of all moral filth and the evil that is so prevalent and humbly accept the word planted in you, which can save you" (James 1:21, NIV). No surgery required!

Day 60

Love is not just a feeling. Love is action. For believers, the action that most shows our love for Jesus is for us to be obedient to His words, His will, and His example. There is no such thing as falling in true love. You actually grow in love and understanding in relationships and God's Word!

Day 61

Some of you are in a battle with the enemy and don't realize it. You think it's your spouse, relative, boss, or coworker, but the battle is in the spirit realm. These obstacles are designed to get you out of the will of God. "For we wrestle not against flesh and blood, but against principalities, against powers, against the rulers of the darkness of this world, against spiritual wickedness in high places" (Ephesians 6:12).

Day 62

There are two types of food: physical and spiritual. You need both to be conquerors! "Jesus answered, 'It is written: *Man does not live on bread alone, but on every word that comes from the mouth of God*" (Matthew 4:4, NIV).

Day 63

If you face an obstacle today so big that you can't see your way out, speak this to your heavenly Father in faith! "Ah, Sovereign Lord, You have made the heavens and the earth by Your great power and outstretched arm. Nothing is too hard for You" (Jeremiah 32:17, NIV).

Day 64

Don't let your current situations and circumstances frustrate you. "He who began a good work in you will carry it on to completion until the day of Christ Jesus" (Philippians 1:6, NIV). If you stay in faith, it must change!

Day 65

Read this slowly: "Now to him who is able to do immeasurably more than all we ask or imagine, according to his power that is at work within us, to him be glory in the church and in Christ Jesus throughout all generations, forever and ever! Amen" (Ephesians 3:20–21, NIV). Let Him blow your mind with His love!

Day 66

Sometimes you need to put your weapons down, hold on to the Word of God and His promise to you. Don't get bogged down in the details of "But when, God?" You are fighting too hard with willpower versus "His power," which is the real power. Just rest in Him and do what the Holy Spirit asks you to do. It might seem silly and simple, but do it anyway!

Day 67

There are some people who read the Bible and say it's very contradictory. It may seem like that in the black and white pages or words, but in the Spirit, it's in perfect harmony from the beginning to the end. You just need more wisdom and understanding (Proverbs 4:7). "As for God, his way is perfect; the word of the Lord is flawless" (Psalms 18:30, NIV).

Day 68

God did not design us to be independent (Sorry, Beyoncé), but rather to be interdependent, especially in the marriage relationship. Both people need to depend on God first, then each other! A lot of people try to glorify being single and independent (that's good for the short term). However, in God's perfect plan, favor is in marriage and relationships. That's why the enemy fights so hard to destroy both!

Day 69

There are people struggling today with situations in which they feel hopeless. Deliverance from adultery, alcohol, porn, abuse, being poor in spirit and/or finances, greed, lust, and pride can be overcome in the Word of God. However, in most cases, it will be a process. Be patient, read the Bible, pray, and regularly attend a Bible-based church!

Day 70

The spiritual state of our nation is in trouble. People, we must put God back in His right place first! If not, we will continue to struggle as a nation with the economy, healthcare, oil crisis, etc. Let's get back to our roots of one nation under God! "Blessed is the nation whose God is the Lord" (Psalms 33:12, NIV).

Day 71

"The heart is deceitful above all things and beyond cure. Who can understand it? I, the Lord, search the heart and examine the mind, to reward a man according to his conduct, according to what his deeds deserve" (Jeremiah 17:9–10, NIV). Like David, even though he made mistakes, he was credited as a man after God's own heart. Don't let your mistakes condemn you!

Day 72

"Do not think of yourself more highly than you ought, but rather think of yourself with sober judgment, in accordance with the measure of faith God has given you" (Romans 12:3, NIV). You ain't all that; I ain't all that; but Jesus is all that and a bag of chips!

Day 73

Sometimes there is no need for a sermon in church. Praise, prayer, and worship may only be necessary to get the Holy Spirit moving to answer prayer, heal, deliver, and set free! Get out of tradition!

Day 74

Lord, please work to bring Yourself glory, not only in me, but in Your people, and in our time of history. Allow Your love to warm the coldest heart today. I pray for Your name to be reverenced in all the earth. Do mighty works that show Your control and sovereignty to help Your people bring others to call on Your name and to praise Your grace.

Day 75

Believe and pray this over yourself today: "The Lord will fulfill his purpose for me; your love, O Lord, endures forever" (Psalms 138:8, NIV).

Day 76

Your level of success is not measured by how much money or things you possess, but rather how many people you positively influence in changing the way they think!

Day 77

I know some of you are wondering with all that's going on in the world what's taking Jesus so long to come back? "The Lord is not slow in keeping his promise, as some understand slowness. He is patient with you, not wanting anyone to perish, but everyone to come to repentance" (2 Peter 3:9, NIV). Yes, He is holding up the process for some rappers, R & B singers, drug dealers, doctors, lawyers, and even some preachers to be saved!

Day 78

We cannot continue to judge people … only God can! The lost need us to show more unconditional love! There is a dying world out there that needs our help and prayers. You have to learn to love people where they are—not what they look like or appear to be. Remember when Jesus defended the woman caught in the very act of adultery when she was getting ready to be stoned? Remember when you were caught in the act of something and should have been *stoned*? It's only by grace and mercy!

Day 79

You may not be feeling very well today. Perhaps you have been very busy and tired. Take a break, but don't give up! The joy of the Lord is your strength! Rejoice in Him and thank Him today for what He has already done for you!

Day 80

The enemy comes to steal, kill, and destroy. Not just physically, but mentally and emotionally. He wants to steal your dreams and hope through sickness, disappointments, and tragedies. He wants to convince you that the word of God does not really work! He is a liar and there is no truth in him!

Day 81

The earnest (heartfelt, continued) prayer of a righteous man makes tremendous power available [dynamic in its working]. You are not righteous by the good things you do! You were made righteous because of the blood of Jesus. Since you were made righteous, God hears and will answer your prayer. Therefore, go boldly to the throne of grace and make your requests known to God!

Day 82

Do you need strength today (physical, emotional, or mental)? No matter what, keep your hope, trust, and confidence in God. Don't even trust yourself! "Those who hope in the Lord will renew their strength. They will soar on wings like eagles; they will run and not grow weary, they will walk and will not be faint" (Isaiah 40:31).

Day 83

Everyone likes to feel important! Make someone feel like a star today! An extraordinary compliment, warm hug, or nice gesture is a good start. Push it further and even do this to those haters (enemies) you have! Build up those spiritual muscles and make the enemy really mad today!

Day 84

Thank God, as a Christian, you have a built-in security system that you don't have to pay for! "The Lord will keep you from all harm—he will watch over your life; the Lord will watch over your coming and going both now and forevermore" (Psalms 121:7–8, NIV). However, I'm not saying to get rid of your ADT and Brink's alarm system if you already have one!

Day 85

You may be going through a tough time now. I have good news! There is no need to fear or be anxious because you have God on your side. Somebody needed to be reminded of that today! "He who dwells in the shelter of the Most High will rest in the shadow of the Almighty" (Psalms 91:1, NIV).

Day 86

Even if you don't know your father like I never knew mine, you have a heavenly Father that knew you while you were in your mother's womb! God loves it when you call Him "Daddy."

Day 87

Now, ladies, the Book says: "Wives, understand and support your husbands in ways that show your support for Christ. The husband provides leadership to his wife the way Christ does to his church, not by domineering, but by cherishing. So just as the church submits to Christ as he exercises such leadership, wives should likewise submit to their husbands" (Ephesians 5:22).

Day 88

"Husbands, go all out in your love for your wives, exactly as Christ did for the church—a love marked by giving, not getting. Christ's love makes the church whole. His words evoke her beauty. Everything he does and says is designed to bring the best out of her. They're really doing themselves a favor—since they're already 'one' in marriage" (Ephesians 5:25).

Day 89

Men do you know how to raise your child/children according to the Word? Here is some insight from Ephesians 6:4: "Fathers, do not irritate and provoke your children to anger [do not exasperate them to resentment], but rear them [tenderly] in the training and discipline and the counsel and admonition of the Lord." Find that fine line of disciplining in love! Spankings are Scriptural if needed!

Day 90

We need to settle this issue in our hearts today: "Because the Sovereign Lord helps me, I will not be disgraced. Therefore, I have set my face like a stone, determined to do his will. And I know that I will not be put to shame" (Isaiah 50:7).

Day 91

Great verse, even for a rapper to use! "The Lord is my light and my salvation; whom shall I fear? The Lord is the strength of my life; of whom shall I be afraid?" (Psalms 27:1). That's hard!

Day 92

Did you know as a Christian you are not only just a U.S. citizen, but a heavenly citizen as well? Oh yeah, through Jesus, you have legal rights to operate like heaven on the earth. Jesus prayed, "Our father which art in heaven thy will be done on earth as it is in heaven." "Our citizenship is in heaven. And we eagerly await a Savior from there, the Lord Jesus Christ" (Philippians 3:20, NIV).

Day 93

Do you like nice gifts? The Holy Spirit is the best gift you can ever receive as a Christian. "If you then, though you are evil, know how to give good gifts to your children, how much more will your Father in heaven give the Holy Spirit to those who ask for him" (Luke 11:13, NIV). Get the Holy Spirit active in your life for wisdom, knowledge, and blessings!

Day 94

There is power in being still! When things happen to you, the first thing innately is to react (mostly negatively). However the word says: "Be still, and know that I am God; I will be exalted among the nations, I will be exalted in the earth" (Psalms 46:10, NIV). Let Him be exalted through you and your issues.

Day 95

God is much bigger than you think and He owns everything! Seek ye first the kingdom of God and all these things will be added unto you! Stretch your faith today!

Day 96

Did somebody just make you upset? Just think how many times you have made God upset with your behavior! You have to forgive them as God through the blood of Jesus has forgiven you! Did you know this could be one reason why you can't get blessed? "Bear with each other and forgive whatever grievances you may have against one another. Forgive as the Lord forgave you" (Colossians 3:13, NIV).

Day 97

The "world's gate" is wide and attractive, but it will mess you up suddenly. God's gate is narrow because it is usually unattractive at first, but it will eventually lead you to true richness. Jesus said, "Wide is the gate and broad is the road that leads to destruction, and many enter through it. But small is the gate and narrow the road that leads to life, and only a few find it" (Matthew 7:13–14, NIV). Choose your road wisely!

Day 98

Pray this today: Lord, thank You for teaching me that true wealth is found in You. Lord, truly, Christ is all that we need. Having a relationship with You will bring the answer to any problem I may face in life. I can trust You to supply all my needs according to Your riches and glory. You promised to take care of me. Lord, help all my friends and family to rest in Your promises, too. I know when I am weak, You are strong! in Jesus's name Amen.

Day 99

People don't go to hell for sinning! That's why Jesus came! They go because they reject Jesus as their Lord and Savior! He is the only one on record that has died and risen again. No other prophet has ever done that! Hell was originally made for Satan and his demons (fallen angels)—not man!

Day 100

Don't change your theology to accommodate your tragedy! God is able and willing for (1) all to be saved (John 3:16), (2) all to be healed (Acts 10:38), (3) all to prosper (Galatians 3:13), and (4) all to be baptized in the Holy Spirit (Acts 1:4). Just because it didn't happen for someone else doesn't mean that it won't happen for you! Some blessing blockers: unforgiveness, pride, selfishness, jealousy, lying, ungratefulness, anger.
—David George

Day 101

Continue to hold on, pray, and believe for your breakthrough! Even though it seems like it is taking forever! God is not bounded by time! "For a thousand years in your sight are like a day that has just gone by, or like a watch in the night" (Psalms 90:4, NIV).

Day 102

"I pray that you, being rooted and established in love, may have power, together with all the saints, to grasp how wide and high and deep is the love of Christ, and to know this love that surpasses knowledge—that you may be filled to the measure of all the fullness of God" (Ephesians 3:17–19, NIV). May his love, filling your heart, wash out your stress today!

Day 103

It is very important when you see others stressed or struggling to help them. It may just be an encouraging word or a good joke to make them laugh. Did you know that laughter is truly medicine? "Encourage one another and build each other up, just as in fact you are doing" (1 Thessalonians 5:11). "A happy heart is good medicine and a cheerful mind works healing, but a broken spirit dries up the bones" (Proverbs 17:22).

Day 104

God owns it all so stop being so selfish! If He wanted to, He could allow your stuff to be taken anytime! "Yours, O Lord, is the greatness and the power and the glory and the majesty and the splendor, for everything in heaven and earth is yours. Yours, O Lord, is the kingdom; you are exalted as head over all" (1 Chronicles 29:11, NIV).

Day 105

Did you know some employers check your Facebook status before they hire you! Make sure whatever you post (profile pictures or comments) represents you in a professional and positive manner—especially if you are looking for employment or trying to keep the job you have!

Day 106

Do you want to be counted wise? Live well and humble. It's the way you live, not the way you talk, that counts! (James 3:13).

Day 107

This is simple, but can be hard—especially in the middle of a disagreement: "A gentle answer turns away wrath, but a harsh word stirs up anger" (Proverbs 15:1, NIV). Sometimes it's better to keep your mouth closed and pray to yourself!

Day 108

I have a friend who was fired one day and rehired by the same company two days later. That's the favor of God! Proverbs 8:35 says, "For whoever finds me finds life and receives favor from the Lord."

Day 109

"Christ was sacrificed once to take away the sins of many people; and he will appear a second time, not to bear sin, but to bring salvation to those who are waiting for him" (Hebrews 9:28, NIV). Ask someone if they know about Jesus today!

Day 110

"Rejoice evermore. Pray without ceasing. In everything, give thanks: for this is the will of God in Christ Jesus concerning you" (1 Thessalonians 5:16–18).

Day 111

I'm telling you today that our God is awesome no matter what your situation looks like! He will show up through anyone or even anything! Did you know that God made a donkey actually talk! (Numbers 22:28). "Then the Lord gave the donkey the ability to speak." Get your faith out there today and expect to hear and receive from Jehovah Jireh (Our Provider). Let's go!

Day 112

This is how it will end for real! "The Lord himself will come down from heaven, with a loud command, with the voice of the archangel and with the trumpet call of God, and the dead in Christ will rise first. After that, we who are still alive and are left will be caught up together with them in the clouds to meet the Lord in the air. And so we will be with the Lord forever" (1 Thessalonians 4:16–17, NIV). Will you be ready?

Day 113

Through all the challenges you face, keep this one close to your heart! "In God, whose word I praise, in God I trust; I will not be afraid. What can mortal man do to me?" (Psalms 56:4, NIV). You are an overcomer through him—no matter what it looks like!

Day 114

"Rejoice with those who rejoice; mourn with those who mourn" (Romans 12:15, NIV). Let's be sensitive to the situations of other people today!

Day 115

A true rebel and gangsta way to live is to live like this: "I consider my life worth nothing to me, if only I may finish the race and complete the task the Lord Jesus has given to me—the task of testifying to the gospel of God's grace" (Acts 20:24, NIV). That's real rebellion because most people are not doing that!

Day 116

No matter what, God's desire is that all will be saved through relationship with Jesus. Don't let this world and all the things in it keep you from the real heavenly world to come. "God did not send his Son into the world to condemn the world, but to save the world through him" (John 3:17, NIV).

Day 117

In marriage, love should not be based on just feelings or what your spouse can do, for you but rather on commitment! Feelings are subject to change by the day, hour, or minute. Commitment is solid like a rock the rock ... Jesus!

Day 118

This one will require training and discipline! "My dear brothers, take note of this: Everyone should be quick to listen, slow to speak and slow to become angry" (James 1:19, NIV). That's why God gave us two ears and one mouth!

Day 119

We really need each other more than we think! "Be devoted to one another in brotherly love. Honor one another above yourselves" (Romans 12:10, NIV). Spend more time honoring and being happy for other people's success versus worrying about just getting yours! Then there would be no room for haters and we all will get to our destination much faster!

Day 120

My God is like helium: He will never let you down!

Day 121

Why do we have so many denominations in our religion? God wants us to be on one accord! "May the God who gives endurance and encouragement give you a spirit of unity among yourselves as you follow Christ Jesus, so that with one heart and mouth, you may glorify the God and Father of our Lord Jesus Christ" (Romans 15:5–6, NIV).

Day 122

Read this slowly! "The wisdom that comes from heaven is first of all pure; then peace-loving, considerate, submissive, full of mercy and good fruit, impartial and sincere. Peacemakers who sow in peace raise a harvest of righteousness" (James 3:17–18, NIV). Get wisdom from heaven—not just earth!

Day 123

Did you know that most hit songs we hear on the radio are really gifts from God to the artists? Unfortunately most are misused! He gifted them to use those beats and those lyrics to glorify him! The angelic choir "kills" all the best rappers, R & B singers, and producers! Think about that!

Day 124

Keep doing good to others—especially to those haters! God will honor you! "God is not unjust; he will not forget your work and the love you have shown him as you have helped his people and continue to help them" (Hebrews 6:10, NIV). Let's go!

Day 125

In Jesus all we do is: win win win win win—no matter what! When that Holy Spirit gets in you, gotta lift your hands up and they stay there and they stay there and they stay there up down up down … up down let's go!

Day 126

"Oh, the depth and riches of the wisdom and the knowledge of God! How unsearchable his judgments, and his paths beyond tracing out" (Romans 11:33, NIV). Wisdom does not necessarily come with age!

Day 127

Do you need the Lord to rejoice over you with singing? Sometimes I do! "The Lord your God is with you, he is mighty to save. He will take great delight in you, he will quiet you with his love, he will rejoice over you with singing" (Zephaniah 3:17, NIV).

Day 128

Don't let the "fine-ness" in that lady mess you up, brothers! You gotta check out the brain and heart too! "Charm is deceptive and beauty is fleeting; but a woman who fears (loves) the Lord is to be praised" (Proverbs 31:30, NIV).

Day 129

Today is a new day, so don't relish in the past! "There is now no condemnation for those who are in Christ Jesus, because through Christ Jesus the law of the Spirit of life in Christ has set me free from the law of sin and death" (Romans 8:1–2, NIV).

Day 130

When someone does you wrong, you must forgive! Why? "Be kind and compassionate to one another, forgiving each other, just as in Christ God forgave you" (Ephesians 4:32, NIV).

Day 131

For some of you, a war may be going on in your life right now. Today sit back and let God fight your battle—not your emotions. Sometimes you need to sit down and shut up! Remember that this is a spiritual battle we are in! Let the spirit of God work today in your situation.

Day 132

What are the characteristics of a godly wife? "A wife of noble character who can find? She is worth far more than rubies. She watches over the affairs of her household and does not eat the bread of idleness. Her children arise and call her blessed; her husband also, and he praises her" (Proverbs 31:10, 27–28, NIV).

Day 133

Be careful how you talk to people. "Make the most of every opportunity. Let your conversation be always full of grace, seasoned with salt, so that you may know how to answer everyone" (Colossians 4:5–6, NIV).

Day 134

When issues come up, don't let them blow you out of God's will for your life. Remember that these are tactics of the enemy. We wrestle not against flesh and blood, but against principalities and evil in higher places. Life is more of a spiritual battle than one in the flesh. Just remember that when someone says or does something to make you mad today, smile at them and the situation to piss the devil off!

Day 135

No matter what, set your spiritual thermostat to love and forgive! God will allow things to happen to build your character. So when these things happen, confuse the devil by praising God. Then you will be building spiritual muscle. "Be joyful always; pray continually; give thanks in all circumstances, for this is God's will for you in Christ Jesus" (1 Thessalonians 5:16-18, NIV).

Day 136

It is not a sin to have an evil thought. An evil thought that comes to our mind is simply the devil tempting us to act upon that thought, which stems from our sinful nature. A thought only becomes sin if we meditate on it, and continue to think on it, until we actually act on it in our heart, and then it manifests in our actions.

Day 137

"Do not be anxious about anything, but in everything, by prayer and petition, with thanksgiving, present your request to God. And the peace of God, which transcends all understanding, will guard your hearts and your minds in Christ Jesus" (Philippians 4:6–7, NIV).

Day 138

The three most difficult things to say are: "I love you," "I'm sorry," and "Help me." Do you fall in any of these categories? I have to admit that I do sometimes!

Day 139

Do you need to be healed or delivered? Be humble, pray, and actively seek godly ways of living. "If my people, who are called by my name, will humble themselves and pray and seek my face and turn from their wicked ways, then will I hear from heaven and will forgive their sin and will heal their land" (2 Chronicles 7:14, NIV).

Day 140

You can't truly be a mature Christian and still believe in luck good or bad!

Day 141

"Be joyful in hope, patient in affliction, faithful in prayer" (Romans 12:12, NIV).

Day 142

Pray this prayer today: Lord, thank you for your hand of correction on my life. I know without it, I would have gone astray and the enemy would have destroyed me. I know you discipline those you love. Lord, help us all to be obedient to your will. Give us a greater desire to serve you and to serve others. Keep us from the evil one. Bless our families and our land. I ask this in the name of the Lord Jesus Christ. Amen.

Day 143

Today, on purpose, replace negatives with positives in every area of your life.

Day 144

Fear robs your confidence and kills your dreams. Hello ... my name is Satan, the creator of fear. Don't I know you?

Day 145

When the light shows up in your struggle, the darkness must flee. Jesus is the light! That means spiritually the situation looks different than before in size, shape, and color. It's suddenly smaller, smoother, and brighter even though it may be still present. When your perception of it changes, then it changes!

Day 146

None of us are perfect! We all have something to work on. Our past has nothing to do with our future! Stop dwelling on the past and get selective amnesia. You are fearfully and wonderfully made!

Day 147

One of the most powerful assets you can have is the ability to influence others to change! However, the prerequisite is for you to be fluid and be able to change as well!

Day 148

Your words impact people! I was getting gas yesterday and someone I did not know said, "Your words on Facebook and Twitter have made a difference in my life!" Wow! Praise God. See, folks, that was what Jesus was talking about spreading. The Gospel not the Gossip!

Day 149

Can you go I-20 east to get to Alabama from Atlanta? Of course not! Well it's the same when you consistently make bad decisions in life. You will end up in a bad destination. Repent and get off on the next exit!

Day 150

Are you stuck in tradition? If so, allow the Holy Spirit and the word of God to be your guide to true freedom! "Therefore do not let anyone judge you by what you eat or drink, or with regard to a religious festival, a New Moon celebration, or a Sabbath day." This describes our freedom in Christ, but not to live recklessly! (Colossians 2:16).

Day 151

The blessing is not the car, house, or money. Those are visible fruits from the tree of God's unseen anointing. The blessing is God's anointing (supernatural power) on your life. This is usually a special gift, talent, or favor that creates the fruits.

Day 152

There is never a dead-end street with God if you have a personal relationship with Jesus. I know that sometimes it may look like that, but like the weather it is subject to change! Jesus is our mediator to God on our behalf and he has never lost a case! He specializes in miracles! We are limited, but he is unlimited!

Day 153

When you accepted Jesus, he placed a deposit in you called the Holy Spirit. He is a guidance counselor strictly for you. He usually speaks to your heart softly and sometimes he instructs you to do things that may not be popular. Popularity doesn't impress God! In fact, it can be wack or lame in his eyes. He is not concerned about your bling, house, or clothes—don't be so dumb!

Day 154

One thing that makes Christianity different from all other religions is hope. Hope is looking to the future for a positive outcome. Our hope is in Jesus! We are guaranteed to live in eternity with God. No other religion can say that! There is evidence that other prophets lived, died, and remains were found. There were no remains found of Jesus because he is now in heaven interceding for us!

Day 155

Think about Christ! He was tired, beaten, and bloody, but nothing could stop His passion. No boundaries, no persecutions, no haters! Not even death! If you're passionate about something, quitting is not an option! How much passion do you have for God and His Word? Even 99 percent isn't enough! My grandma said she gotta make 100 because 99 ½ won't do!

Day 156

He forgives your sins—every one.
He heals your diseases—every one.
He redeems you from hell—saves your life!
He crowns you with love and mercy—a paradise crown.
He wraps you in goodness—beauty eternal.
His name is Jesus!

Day 157

Today, speak to your mountain instead of about it. With your natural or spiritual eye, look at it and verbally command it to be removed. Jesus did this when he spoke to the fig tree. This requires faith and is different than prayer. Your mountain will respond better to your voice when it is activated by faith and love!

Day 158

Some of you are still holding on to hurt. I know it's hard to let go, but you must in order to be more effective for the kingdom of God. Love like you have never been hurt!

—Jentezen Franklin

Day 159

How much power do you want from God to do exploits for him? Well, it depends on three things: Your level of (1) love, (2) faith, and (3) obedience. Satan knows this as well and that's why he creates distractions to keep you from this power. It's time for us to rise up in the power and glory of his might!

Day 160

Sometimes people are concerned about sinners who seemingly are not suffering for the wicked things they have done to others. Please don't let this worry you. God will judge and punish them sooner or later. Our job as Christians is to pray for them and hopefully they will come to God with a truly repentant heart. Eventually to become saved through Jesus!

Day 161

A faith that has not been tested can't be trusted! Some people talk about having faith, but have not yet been tested or challenged with a situation in which they had no answers. Completely relying on God is the way to a passing grade! Have you had your faith tested lately? If so, did you pass?

—Bishop T.D. Jakes

Day 162

Don't let feelings direct your emotions. As humans, we are emotional by nature, which can get you in a lot of trouble! However, as a Christian, you have a blood-bought right to take authority over the feeling and do what's right. This takes practice (repetitiveness even if you keep falling). This ultimately becomes a heart-and-mind-over-matter issue.

Day 163

We all go through trials and tribulations in life even as seasoned Christians. Don't beat yourself up because you are not perfect or have not been delivered yet! God is more concerned about how you finish versus coming in first place!

Day 164

Right now, Christian marriages are under attack! Yes, at times I know you want to trade in your spouse for a new one like a car, but you may get stuck with a lemon. Some of your marriages just need a tune-up and some may need to be overhauled. Whatever your case, pray and love one another and let God do the rest.

Day 165

Did you know as a child of God you have your own Secret Service? Yes! You have angels that are assigned to assist you in fulfilling your God-given purpose on this earth. "He ordered his angels to guard you wherever you go. If you stumble, they'll catch you; their job is to keep you from falling" (Psalms 91:11–12).

Day 166

God calls Christians to love unconditionally (agape)—everyone—no matter the race, religion, or culture. Once enough of us really put this into practice, we will see more people come to Christ! Christ loved you while you were unlovely.

Day 167

So, whatever challenge you're faced with, don't give up. It's a fight all your life. It doesn't matter how many times you fall; get up! One of these times, you're going to get the victory over that temptation and live the life you were called to do!

Day 168

I want to encourage you today. Don't let the enemy steal where you are to be blessed. I was the only African American dentist in my area. When I first opened my practice, it was vandalized. I wanted to leave, but God told me to stay because this is where he was to bless and sustain me. I listened and more than six years later, we are still growing!

Day 169

Your relationship with God grows more by just showing up versus performance alone. Show up in church, in prayer, in giving, in loving, in faithfulness, in kindness, in gentleness, in self-control, and in patience. Just show up in God's presence and don't worry about just making the grade! Stay moldable and he will change you and take the stress off changing yourself.

Day 170

Don't let people manipulate your Christian faith to strong-arm or softly persuade you into doing things that you don't want to do or are called to do. It's okay to try the unknown, but if it's not working for you, nicely let the other person know. Unfortunately, there are Christian people out there that will try to make you feel guilty when you say no. These may be colleagues, family, or friends.

Day 171

I was eating sushi the other day and an Asian guy said, "If this pastor did that to those boys, then see there is no God!" Lord, I ask you today to show your goodness and mercy. Reveal yourself to those who don't believe in you. Empower and give strength to those who love you in Jesus's name. Amen.

Day 172

Today, I dare you to say, "I love Jesus!" to somebody you don't know. Are you up for this simple challenge? Let's go!

Day 173

See, young world, this is what I am talking about. You can be highly educated, love God, and still be cool! Now what?

Day 174

We must learn how to give by the Spirit's direction and not allow our emotions or sympathy to rule us. We should not give mechanically to people or events because it has been our pattern in times past, but we should remain open to the Lord's direction for our giving as with all guidance. Sometimes the Lord may speak that we are not to give to a certain person or ministry at a particular time.

Day 175

"God is not my financial advisor; He is my financial commander." How many people can say that? Rich is relative; greed is diverse; and wealth is uncertain. Who do you trust with your money?

Day 176

Most of the people of Israel have not found the favor of God they are looking for so earnestly. A few have—the ones God has chosen. They were disobedient, so God made salvation available to the Gentiles (non-Jews). He wanted his own people to become jealous of the life we live and claim it for themselves (belief that Jesus is the Messiah) so some may be saved (Romans 11:9–1).

Day 177

Would you rather have money or influence? I hope you choose influence because, with proper and godly influence, you can always make money.

Day 178

I had a thirty-five year-old patient today who admitted that he had a phobia about brushing his teeth for years. Recently, he said he spent thousands of dollars to get psycho-hypnosis to be able to brush! Wow! Please pray for others besides yourself!

Day 179

Jesus said that he came for the sick—not the healthy! I have realized that the church is a spiritual hospital. Every now and then, we all need to go in for a check-up! When was the last time you had yours?

Day 180

We must not allow the devil to use our mouths to speak evil things that bring destruction on ourselves and others, especially before we hear the truth of the matter. Even if that person sinned (missed the mark), it is our job as Christians to love, accept, and forgive just as Jesus has done so many times for us!

Day 181

God listens to a person with an honest heart and will not turn the most wicked and vile person away from salvation if they come to Him with a repentant and honest heart. However, based on the sin committed, there is an earthly cost to pay. Lord, help us to always be honest and never try to pretend or put on a show to impress others.

Day 182

Just as the mustard seed grew into a tree, the kingdom message grows inside you once it is planted. That is why it's important to expose children to the Word at a young age! When they get older (spiritually mature), they will come back when God calls them. Once a seed is planted, God makes it grow and, yes, it needs to be watered—but not necessarily by you!

Day 183

I was praying this morning about my business and finances. God revealed to me that bills are purposed to bless somebody else's business—just as your business is blessed when patients come to see you! He also said about finances: We may run low, but we will never run out because of His anointing on your life!

Day 184

Jesus said, "But go and learn what this means: 'I desire mercy, not sacrifice.' For I have not come to call the righteous, but sinners" (Matthew 9:13, NIV).

Day 185

Unforgiveness plus bitterness equals a spiritual midget. Have you checked your height lately?

Day 186

No one has ever choked when swallowing their pride!
—Author Unknown

Day 187

When your mate or spouse says something such as "It feels like I'm getting fat," instantly tell them that you love them! The issue is usually deeper than weight and a scale. It's really needing affirmation of love! That scale is a liar like Satan anyway! Take time to encourage someone today with something positive! Let's go!

Day 188

Do you know the secret formula for peace? Pray + ask + thank = peace! (Philippians 4:4–7).

Day 189

God gifted Solomon with the ability to not only to write, but to compose music as well. Today God is also gifting many with this same ability so that we all may be blessed. Unfortunately, Satan has used some of these gifts to deceive us, especially some hip-hop and R & B music. Some of these lyrics are designed to destroy us!

Day 190

My daughter left church singing "God is bigger than the Boogie Man." Amazing! I think some adults need to sing and believe that too!

Day 191

"The godly man may trip seven times in one day, but they will get up again" (Proverbs 24:16, NLT).

Day 192

"Proclaim further: This is what the Lord Almighty says: 'My towns will again overflow with prosperity, and the Lord will again comfort Zion and choose Jerusalem.'" Don't get discouraged, child of God! Keep speaking your future into your present! (Zechariah 1:17, NIV).

Day 193

Success breeds envy! Boy, the haters gonna really be mad at me! Don't matter because I'm rolling with The Great I AM! How about you? Ha! Let's go!

Day 194

Okay, folks, by now, you should realize that debt is your enemy! Quit eating out all the time, buying new clothes, and just hanging out if your bills aren't paid! It will come back to bite you in the rear end!

Day 195

My four-year-old daughter Jayla said, "Daddy, I want to be a doctor!" I said, "Great. You can be just like your daddy." She said, "No, daddy—a doctor, not a dentist!" Humbly, I said, "You don't need to be either to give healing to hurting people."

Day 196

"And God is able to make all grace (every favor and earthly blessing) come to you in abundance, so that you may always and under all circumstances and whatever the need be self-sufficient" (2 Corinthians 9:8). This means possessing enough to require no aid or support and being furnished in abundance for every good work and charitable donation.

Day 197

It is so refreshing to see so many friends and sometimes old foes come to Christ. Who would have ever known that God could save some of those folks—including me!

Day 198

I've come to realize how significant having a covenant marriage (esteeming God as the main source) really is! God honors and blesses that type of marriage! There is no way that I could have become so successful so fast if it was not for my wife, Angela. She is truly a wife of noble character! If you feel the same way about your spouse, tell her today!

Day 199

"My little children, I write you these things so that you may not violate God's law and sin. But if anyone should sin, we have an Advocate (One who will intercede for us) with the Father—[it is] Jesus Christ [the all] righteous [upright, just, who conforms to the Father's will in every purpose, thought, and action]" (1 John 2:1, AMP).

Day 200

"What marvelous love the Father has extended to us! Just look at it—we're called children of God! That's who we really are. But that's also why the world doesn't recognize us or take us seriously, because it has no idea who he is or what he's up to" (1 John 3:1, MSG).

Day 201

"Give, and it shall be given unto you; good measure, pressed down, and shaken together, and running over, shall men give into your bosom. For with the same measure that ye mete withal it shall be measured to you again" (Luke 6:38). This scripture can really bless you or really hurt you—depending on what type of seed you are sowing (good or bad).

Day 202

To all the holy rollers: Our problem is not just the music artists themselves, but our common enemy: Satan! He actually uses them through the lure of money, power, and sex to become his puppets! (1 John 2:1, NIV).

Day 203

As humans, we all have a common enemy: Satan! He will not show up as a goblin with a pitchfork, but as something very beautiful or exotic to entice or seduce your mind, will, and emotions! (2 Samuel 22:38, NIV).

Day 204

David said, "For I have kept the ways of the Lord; I have not done evil by turning from my God." How can a murderer and adulterer say this? I believe he repented and admitted his sins to God thereby purifying his heart quickly. How much more forgiveness we have in the blood of Jesus!

Day 205

The spirit of gossip is running rampant in homes, offices, and churches today. Gossip is mean-spirited and stealth in its attack. Like a small cancer with no symptoms, if left unchecked, it will become deadly.

Day 206

When situations arise in your life and you don't know the answer, pray first! If there is no answer, be patient—and don't get mad! People get messed up by getting impatient and moving too fast, which usually puts them out of the will of God. The funny thing is that they tend to blame God for things not working out instead of themselves. He will provide if He is in it!

Day 207

Is asking for positive energy a politically correct word for prayer? Hmmm.

Day 208

We are not at war with Islam or any other religion, but rather with extremist who takes the lives of innocent people and tries to justify it by twisting religion. The USA is founded on solid constitutional rights and one is the freedom of religion. This makes us very special and one reason why God has blessed us!

Day 209

Any act performed out of hatred is ungodly—even if it seems to be righteous. For example, burning the American flag or the Quran. God is more concerned with relationship than religion. A true relationship with God is based in love, not hate. Do you love others that don't look the same as you or have different religious beliefs?

Day 210

If you were to die today, would you want to be remembered by what you post on Facebook or Twitter? What kind of words are you leaving behind for your children and others? Think about that today.

Day 211

As a God-loving American, you should support and pray for every president in office. This is our responsibility as American citizens. Yes, I understand that we won't agree on every issue, but that's the beauty of our democracy! Safety is trusting in God not in man! "The fear of man brings a snare: but whoever puts his trust in the Lord shall be safe" (Proverbs 29:25).

Day 212

To have change, you must change! Things can't be done the same way anymore. Change is not easy, but it is necessary for advancement. Change the way you think and value other people's opinion—even if you don't agree with it. There is always something you can learn. We all are influenced by our upbringing and surroundings.

Day 213

"He said to His disciples, 'Why are you so afraid? Do you still have no faith?'" Sometimes we get like that when storms come into our lives! Jesus tells us not to worry because He is in control—so don't jump ship! Trust in him today and forevermore! (Mark 4:40, TNIV).

Day 214

Without a divine call, no one can be saved. We are all so sunk in sin, and so wedded to the world, that we would never turn to God and seek salvation unless He first called us by His grace. God must speak to our hearts by His Spirit, before we shall ever speak to Him.

—J. C. Ryle

Day 215

God does not waste any of your pain or wrong decisions. They are all recycled to make new things in Him for someone else. We in the church are just recycled goods made new in Jesus. Thank God that we are never thrown away like trash, but can always be recycled because of the blood of Jesus!

Day 216

In life, there will be challenges to face whether you believe in God or not! However for his anointed ones (people dedicated to the things of God), there will always be victory in the end!

Day 217

As Christians, we must learn how to stay in the pocket like a quarterback when the pressure is on! Sure, you may get hit and even sacked a few times, but those hits will make you stronger and more confident in the future. Eventually you will stand with patience and assurance to see downfield and throw the winning touchdown!

Day 218

Prayer for today: "Oh, Lord, Keep your servant from deliberate sins! Don't let them control me. Then I will be free of guilt and innocent of great sin." This was one of King David's prayers! Make it one of yours if you are struggling with sin! (Psalms 19:13, NLT).

Day 219

I know that sometimes you think, *Lord, I know your word says this, but look at what they did to me!* "The instructions of the Lord are perfect, reviving the soul. The decrees of the Lord are trustworthy, making wise the simple." Trust him! (Psalms 19:7, NLT).

Day 220

True deliverance is not running from or avoiding your problems, but running toward and through your problems. Today, stare that problem in the face and tell it by faith: "You are defeated by the blood of Jesus. Whether I am delivered now or later, I know that I will be free!"

Day 221

All good gifts come from above. "I said to the Lord, 'You are my master! Every good thing I have comes from you.'" God, I thank you for the gift of healing in the area of root canal therapy. I don't take credit for being known as the pain-free root canal specialist. You deserve it all! (Psalms 16:2, NLT).

Day 222

Lord, I pray for those who are struggling with a particular area of sin in their lives. Send your mercy and grace to them right now. That stronghold will be broken and your anointing will flow through them to get others free. Lord, others see our actions, but only you know their hearts. Help them now, Lord Jesus!

Day 223

Are you tired of reading about the same authors writing the same stuff about steps to this and get that, keys to this and get that, do this and get that? God very seldom works out a foolproof map to fix everyone's problems the same way. Our battles will be different at various times. However, the Lord will hold our hand through every one of them—so don't get discouraged. Let's go!

Day 224

Lord, I was just thinking about how much You love me. You took a kid who has never seen his dad from a single-parent household with no formal education, who was around drugs, premarital sex, abusive relationships, violence, homosexuality in family, superstition, and dependent upon the government for support. Like Kirk Franklin says: Look at me now! I just wanted to say thank you and to encourage someone else whose background may be similar or worse. Remember that it's not where you come from, but where you are going!

Day 225

Some people have perspective distortion (a warping of an object and its surrounding area that differs significantly from what the object would normally look like). They pay attention to what others have without knowing their risks to keep it. The phrase "Objects in mirror are closer than they appear" on the right side of your car is an example of this illusion. Be careful to stay in your own lane!

Day 226

Today, let us all move forward in the things of God. Forgetting about the past and pulling our future into our present!
—Bishop Jim Bolin

Day 227

Everyone talks about change, which is great. However, I think it's better if we are transformed. Sometimes when things are changed, they have the capacity to go back to their natural state once enough stress is added or removed. Being transformed is to change in composition and structure permanently like a caterpillar changing into a butterfly!

Day 228

Be careful to observe the real meaning of certain holidays. Take Halloween, for example. Halloween originally is a celebration meant for being thankful for the end of the harvest season and all Saints Day. Somehow this was changed to trick or treating and fears of ghosts and evil spirits. Remember that God did not give us the spirit of fear! He gave us power, love, and a sound mind.

Day 229

Today I want to encourage you to remember that in God you are strong (Jehovah Nissi—your banner of protection—Psalms 27:1). He is your Jehovah Jireh (Provider). Take your eyes off the situation and fix them on Jesus. How do you do that? Just think about the many times he made a way out of no way for you! Start praising and rejoicing because if he did it once, he can do it again.

Day 230

Happiness is subject to change, but joy is a permanent daily choice!

Day 231

I know that sometimes you don't feel like being positive. You may be tired or worried about something today. No matter what, you must continue to move forward in a positive direction. In fact, the times when I don't feel like posting on Facebook or lifting up others is usually when the most people are encouraged! Do you think Jesus felt like dying on the cross? No! But he did it anyway—not for himself, but for you and me.

Day 232

When the enemy comes in like a flood, the Lord will lift up a standard against him! However, you must give him permission through prayer! Be encouraged today!

Day 233

1 Chronicles 4:10 talks about the Prayer of Jabez: "He was the one who prayed to the God of Israel, 'Oh, that you would bless me and expand my territory! Please be with me in all that I do, and keep me from all trouble and pain!' And God granted him his request." Keep that prayer in your arsenal!

Day 234

The greatest man in history, Jesus, had no servants, yet they called Him Master. Had no degree, yet they called Him Teacher. Had no medicines, yet they called Him Healer. He had no army, yet kings feared Him. He won no military battles, yet he conquered the world. He committed no crime, yet they crucified Him. He was buried in a tomb, yet he lives today.

—Author Unknown

Day 235

One day, my daughter asked, "Daddy, how old is the devil?" I told her that I'm not quite sure, but old enough to know about his name: "d–evil" one!

Day 236

Pray this prayer today: "Lord, You have blessed me so much compared to many in the world and may I be sensitive to the needs of the poor. Lord, I do not want to be guilty of turning a deaf ear to the cries of those who are hungry. Direct my giving, and create a heart of generosity within me, so that I can be used as an instrument of blessing to the many needy in this world."

—Bible.com

Day 237

Have you ever been caught doing something wrong? That's a bad feeling, right? Usually there was punishment associated with it as well! There was a woman caught in the act of adultery. "And Jesus said unto her, neither do I condemn thee: go, and sin no more" (John 8:11). Wow! He is ready to forgive you for your sins—not condemn you!

Day 238

There are marriages under attack right now. I pray: Lord, deliver Your people from the spirit of divorce. Ungodly divorce is cowardly and selfish. So what if your spouse made you mad ... pray and get over it! We are designed for a relationship (man and woman) since the beginning. May we look to You, Father, and other godly examples of marriage for the sake of our children. Lord, in every home, allow wives to submit to their husbands and husbands to cherish and love their wives. In Jesus's name. Amen.

Day 239

Christians, quit judging people's salvation based on how they look or what they have done in the past! Your job is to love and pray for them unconditionally. Let God be the judge!

Day 240

Time is out on traditionally voting democrat or republican! Look at the candidate's godly character and what they stand for or against. We are in a new age where candidates can camouflage themselves to sway voters to push their own agenda once elected. The Bible says that when the godly are in authority, the people will rejoice!

Day 241

Lord, I pray for those Christians who are stuck in a sinful habit. Allow your grace and mercy to cover them today. There is no condemnation for those in Christ Jesus. Your plan is to give them hope and a prosperous future. Devil, you are a liar! Jesus is coming back for a spotless church and we will be spotless because of His blood!

Day 242

Did someone make you upset and you want to get even? Dear friends, never take revenge. Leave that to the righteous anger of God. For the Scriptures say, "I will take revenge; I will pay them back, says the Lord" (Romans 12:19). He can do it better!

Day 243

Pray for people in positions of power—whether Godly or not. Ask the Holy Spirit to reveal to you God's established authority. Support rulers that promote good works and resist those that promote evil.

Day 244

Quit waiting around for a handout from your church and get to work! Ask not what your church can do for you, but what you can do for your church!

Day 245

The Church is now mostly divided, angry, and frustrated. Old tradition of "playing church" is over. People need to see genuine people who reflect the image of God. Not in perfection but in love, acceptance, and forgiveness. Then you will see more people in the world wanting to know more about this "Jesus guy."

Day 246

Don't fool yourself! Willpower alone is not permanent! You can't get yourself right! "For God is working in you, giving you the desire and the power to do what pleases him" (Philippians 2:13, NLT).

Day 247

If you are a born-again Christian, "God has now reconciled you to himself through the death of Christ in his physical body. As a result, he has brought you into his own presence, and you are holy and blameless as you stand before him without a single fault." The blood of Jesus! (Colossians 1:22, NLT).

Day 248

Don't be so easily shaken or alarmed by those who say that the day of the Lord has already begun. Don't believe them—even if they claim to have had a spiritual vision, a revelation, or a letter supposedly from us. Don't be fooled by what they say. For that day will not come until there is a great rebellion against God and the man of lawlessness is revealed.—The Bible

Day 249

The Antichrist described: This man will come to do the work of Satan with counterfeit power and signs and miracles. He will use every kind of evil deception to fool those on their way to destruction, because they refuse to love and accept the truth that would save them. No red suit and pitchfork! Sorry!

Day 250

Most people don't want to hear the truth. They just want someone to tell them something to justify their actions. I believe that the stage is being set for the Antichrist now. Look at the media and politics. "Let's just try to make everybody happy" is one example of the slick methods he will use.

Day 251

One way that we can make going to church more attractive to the young folks is to be real with them! We need to share our personal stories from our past instead of trying to be "holier than thou" and fake!

Day 252

Imagine being on a team such as the Lakers with Kobe Bryant. He has won numerous championships. Others on the team that received little or no recognition got a ring too. Jesus is like our Kobe Bryant, Michael Jordan, and Lebron James mixed together—on steroids! With him on our team, it is a sure win—even though some of us may occasionally sit on the bench!

Day 253
Wisdom is engaging knowledge at the proper time!

Day 254
Life is not easy—as if you haven't figured that out yet. Satan is always seeking to gain the advantage over us. Sometimes it's not the big sins, but rather those small ones that others don't know about, that are the most dangerous! Like undiagnosed cancer, they can kill us if they remain untreated! However, we do not stand alone in our battle against Satan. God has given us Jesus and his Holy Spirit in our hearts. They guarantee the final victory.

Day 255

As a Christian, people need to see us in action not just in word! Our wrong lives will drown out our right words. We need to live true lives as well as true words. Lord, help us to reflect you in all our ways (both publicly and privately) so that we can draw others to you! In Jesus's name. Amen.

Day 256

We all know that most New Year's resolutions fizz out quickly. Having a relationship with Jesus is the best New Year's resolution you can ever make!

Day 257

At home, what kind of person are you? Do you put on a front for your boss, coworkers, or friends? If so, once you get more stuff (promotion, money, fame, etc.) it will be even harder to wear the mask. Money and fame tend to amplify who you really are! Yes, including your habits and addictions—sometimes even leading to an early death! Are you still ready to be famous? If so, get wisdom!

Day 258

Ever wondered why some good, godly people die so young? Isaiah 57 gives us one answer—to spare them from more worldly trouble and pain. As Christians, earth is not our real home. Our real home is in heaven with God. When we (the godly) die, we will be in peace hence RIP (Rest in Peace). However, when people die who are not godly, the same does not apply. Torture never ends (TNE)!

Day 259

There are people who use the Word of God just to make money for themselves (the love of money is the root of evil) and there are really pulpit pimps out there! There are even some members that try to buy the spiritual gifts of the pastor! Beware! Peter said, "To hell with your money! And you along with it. Why, that's unthinkable—trying to buy God's gift!"

Day 260

Today, work on turning negative energy into positive energy! You can do it! It starts with your words!

Day 261

Let's get refocused this year. God wants to give us something more important than money—wisdom! Money automatically shows up when wisdom is employed. "Prefer my life-disciplines over chasing after money, and God-knowledge over a lucrative career." Jesus was not employed, but was rich! However, for our sakes, he became poor so that we might be rich—the righteousness of God! (Proverbs 8:10).

Day 262

"This is how much God loved the world: He gave his Son, His one and only Son. And this is why: so that no one need be destroyed; by believing in him, anyone can have a whole and lasting life." Wow! Did you catch that, anyone? Jesus joins everyone together (Christians, Muslims, Hindus, Buddhists, Jews, etc.) on one accord with God. No other prophet can say or do that! (John 3:16, MSG).

Day 263

Jesus knew since we were born in sin that it's not just the devil that causes us to sin, but our very human nature. So we can't go around blaming the devil for everything. However, God has devised a plan for all sin—no matter what the root source is, which is the blood of Jesus! On your very best day, you can be good but not God (sinless). It is impossible being sinless all by yourself! There are some sins that you commit and are not even aware of them. That's why we need the blood of Jesus every day! I'm not talking about just religion, but rather relationship. Jesus had a relationship with God—not just a bunch of ritualistic ideas or actions. This means open communication with God in prayer. He wants to hear from you today (Luke 11:4).

Day 264

There will be situations and circumstances that family and friends will come against you because you are blessed (haters). Relax! The favor of God isn't fair! Don't be afraid of them and don't stop talking to them. Keep loving them as if nothing has happened! Don't apologize or feel bad. The blessing of God is on your life!

Day 265

Don't wait for the light to show up in the room! You show up in the room and light it up! Let's go!

Day 266

As a Christian, sin waters down your swagger!

Day 267

Did you know that there were other miracles Jesus performed that were not recorded in the Bible? "There are so many other things Jesus did. If they were all written down, each of them, one by one, I can't imagine a world big enough to hold such a library of books." I want to stunt like my daddy! (John 21:25, MSG).

Day 268

Your works may go unnoticed with people, but not with God. He sees everything—so keep doing good whether you get earthly credit or not! "God doesn't require attention-getting devices. He won't overlook what you are doing; He'll reward you well (Matthew 6:18).

Day 269

Do you want a six pack for your abs? Guess what? You already have one! It is just covered up! In order to see it, it must be developed through diet and exercise! The same is true with your spiritual life. Once you become a child of God by accepting Jesus, he has deposited everything in you to become an overcomer. It just has to be developed by reading, praying, and obeying his word!

Day 270

A truly wise person will admit when he or she is wrong. Change directions and move forward—no matter what!

Day 271

From scripture, the Muslims and Jews have the same father (Abraham), but different mothers (Hagar—Ishmael mother—Muslim nation) and (Sarah—Isaac mother—Jewish nation), which makes them actually half-brothers! So what is all the fighting about? The inheritance (land, money, power)? Jesus came from the blood lineage of Abraham too, through Sarah and Isaac. See, Jesus comes into place to bring everyone together into a brand-new family. He does not care what race, religion, or country you were born in. It does not matter! When you accept him as your Lord and Savior, you are reborn into a new family … God's family. So therefore, fighting for things and positions does not matter once you are a Christian. Your inheritance is guaranteed because of what Jesus did … which is eternal life … the ultimate inheritance! The other stuff you can't take with you when you die anyway! Jesus unites us as one big family and is gonna throw us a huge party once we get to heaven!

Day 272

Quit putting God in a box. He created everything and can solve any problem. "'Dear God, my Master, you created earth and sky by your great power—by merely stretching out your arm! There is nothing you can't do" (Jeremiah 32:17, MSG).

Day 273

Have you ever heard of the age of accountability? Basically, it is the age when you have to pay for your own sins because you are now old enough. Before the age of accountability, your parents were charged. This is where I believe that idea came from: "By the time the child is twelve years old, able to make moral decisions " (Isaiah 7:15, MSG). Interesting, but I think it is used out of context. Once you are saved, Jesus's blood takes care of all that once and for all!

Day 274

But you, Timothy (or fill in your name), man of God: Run for your life from all this (worldly stuff). Pursue a righteous life—a life of wonder, faith, love, steadiness, courtesy." That's our goal! (1 Timothy 6:11, MSG).

Day 275

Can you truly love God and love money equally? "Lust for money brings trouble and nothing but trouble. Going down that path, some lose their footing in the faith completely and live to regret it bitterly ever after" (1 Timothy 6:10, MSG). Running hard—but backward!

Day 276

Are you married or have been to a wedding? If so, you know how important that wedding dress is, right? It has to look elegant, fit perfectly, and be spotless on that special day. This is the same idea when we are referred to as the bride of the Christ which is his church. Because of His blood, we will put on that beautiful spotless wedding dress that represents his righteousness that washes our sin away. Notice that this is not a covering, but a complete removal … there is nothing to show through! Historically, in a wedding, the gown is pure white to represents purity like a virgin. We can never be pure in and of our own selves because we were born into sin. Before we had a choice, sin was already there! But thanks be to God, He had a plan through Jesus. The only way we can be pure (like the white wedding gown) is by accepting Him as our lord and savior. And now to the wedding feast or party! Look back to when you were at someone's wedding reception. Sometimes it was more extravagant than the ceremony itself! Just imagine what God will have on his menu and entertainment when we get there! Did you get your invitation yet? If not, there is still space available. This is how: (1) Acknowledge that you are a sinner and are in need of a savior. (2) Believe that Jesus died, was buried, and rose for your sins. (3) Ask him to come in and be Lord over your life. You will be seated at table ____.

Day 277

The best of Christians are poor frail people, and need the blood of Jesus for forgiveness and prayer every day of their lives. Don't let some self-righteous religious person fool you! We would be nothing without the sacrificial blood of Jesus!

Day 278

Anything whereby we may glorify God is a talent. All that we have is a loan from God. To hide our talent is to neglect opportunities to glorify God when we have them. We and God must one day meet face to face. We shall have to render an account of every privilege that was granted to us, and of every ray of light that we enjoyed. What will you say?

Day 279

Have you ever wondered why it seems like the people with the most money are not God's people? This morning he answered in my spirit. "They are usually further from me and my will than people who have less, which places them at a disadvantage actually! They trust in their money more than me. I feel sorry for them when that time comes. Yes, that party will end—and then what?" Thank you, Father, for giving me insight!

Day 280

Go shopping for someone that is not a part of your immediate family such as a patient in a nursing home or hospital, your mail carrier, your garbage collector, a foster child, or even that coworker that does not like you! Watch and see what happens! Jesus said, "If you love those who love you, what good is that?" Let's go together!

Day 281

Even the government back in the day was smart enough to trust in God and not just in themselves! Our government needs to get back to some of the principles on which it was founded! On our money, it says "In God We Trust!" Let's trust Him today!

Day 282

The economy, presidential issues, taxes, etc. are mere child's play to God! He just wants all of us to ask him, seek him, and trust him for help. Remember that our currency says, "In God We Trust."

Day 283

Consider the eagle, one of the most valiant birds and a symbol that represents the strength of the United States. Storms create the best wind drafts, so he flies the best when the winds are contrary. The Bible uses the eagle to describe "overcoming Christians" because we can also fly above any storm of life by mounting up in the presence of God!

Day 284

Satan is like the class clown student trying to distract and disrupt the rest of the class. He has failed the course already anyway! Don't let him distract you. With the Holy Spirit as our tutor and counselor, we will pass this test of life and graduate into eternity with our heavenly peers!

Day 285

We all will face testing in this life. Some tests more challenging than others. But God has given us the cheat sheet through Jesus. So the next time you feel like you did not pass (and maybe you didn't!), be encouraged. There will be a retake coming up. The Holy Spirit will prepare us to pass—so don't worry!

Day 286

Have you ever noticed Christmas lights around you? You can't see them well during the day, but at night, they shine bright with many wonderful colors. In fact, the darker it is outside, the more beautiful and brighter they shine! Well, that's how it is in the world today. The darker the world gets, the more beautiful and brighter the people of God will shine. Perhaps it's not as dark as we think it is!

Day 287

Our mentor and teacher, the ultimate straight-A "Sinless Student" is Jesus. He will be present in the class of life, whispering the answers in our ear. While all along, God is the dean and creator of the school called "Life."

Day 288

Do you believe in demons? Jesus points out there are different kind of demons with different jobs just as there are different kinds of angels (messenger, warring, etc.). So there are some demonic spirits that can be cast out easier than others. There was a particular one that the disciples were not familiar with. Perhaps they had some fears which led to some unbelief which led to some "loss of power." Jesus mentioned prayer and fasting being able to cast some demonic kinds out. Could he have meant praying in tongues (heavenly gifted languages) as well ... The perfect prayer? I think that he was trying to train the disciples about what to do when he would no longer physically be present with them.

Day 289

Most people want instant success. The problem is that if they rise to the top too fast, they can fall just as fast! God promotes with precision and judges your heart. What he promotes, he will sustain. In God's kingdom, the way to the top is sometimes down first. He has to establish your roots so you can be strong when the storm comes. Being a servant first allows your roots to be established so you will know what to do once appointed a king! Let's go together!

Day 290

A lot of people are trying to live in two worlds. They know what is true. They effectively believe it is true. But they have not turned from darkness to light. Have you turned from darkness to light? Are you following Jesus Christ? Or are you just going to church?

Day 291

A warning to all manipulating ministers: "On the other hand, if you give one of these simple, childlike believers a hard time, bullying or taking advantage of their simple trust, you'll soon wish you hadn't. You'd be better off dropped in the middle of the lake with a millstone around your neck" (Mark 9).

Day 292

What is greatness? In God's view, greatness is not about what I accomplish—my gifts are all from Him so it's not mine to claim anyway! Greatness is about character, attitude, and loving my neighbor as myself. It is about helping others become what God has created them to be and not striving for power or authority over them. It is about seeking God above all else and leaving my own needs aside for him to provide.

Day 293

When we read about Jesus's family line, we see a liar in Jacob and a prostitute in Rahab, yet that is His family tree. They—along with others—encountered God at some point that changed their lives. Don't look at your family tree and sell yourself short! God specializes in using ordinary, messed up people to do extraordinary things! God wants to do something radically ridiculous in your life today. Let him in!

Day 294

The death rate for human beings hovers right around 100 percent, and is expected to remain there for well, forever. Consider this: if the average lifespan is seventy-seven years, then that means we only have seventy-seven summers seventy-seven winters seventy-seven Christmas mornings seventy-seven New Years, and that's it. Live, love, laugh like it's your last!

—Author Unknown

Day 295

In ancient Rome, people used decorative wreaths as a sign of victory. Some believe that this is where the hanging of wreaths on doors came from. In Christ, we have the victory and the thorn of crowns he wore possibly represented the wreath!

Day 296

Advent comes from the Latin word *adventus,* meaning arrival or coming. Traditionally, Advent counts down the four weeks leading up to Christmas. Practically, Advent reminds us to look forward to His return every day! No man—not even the Son of Man (Jesus)—knows the day or hour!

Day 297

As servants of God, we must work firmly but patiently with those who refuse to obey. You never know how or when God might sober them up with a change of heart and a turning to the truth," We must continue to pray for the nonbeliever. We too once did not really believe (2 Timothy 2:25, MSG).

Day 298

But the time is coming—it has, in fact, come—when what you're called will not matter and where you go to worship will not matter. "It's who you are and the way you live that count before God. Your worship must engage your spirit in the pursuit of truth. That's the kind of people the Father is out looking for: those who are simply and honestly themselves before him in their worship" (John 4:23, MSG).

Day 299

Jesus and Paul used the word "church" in reference to the people of God. Church never referred to a religious building.

Day 300
Family and true friends are important! "Friends love through all kinds of weather, and families stick together in all kinds of trouble" (Proverbs 17:17, MSG).

Day 301
This is the Christian life in a nutshell, we have victory or revelation in our lives only because of God, and then the next moment we fall on our faces (sin). God has to pick us up and scrape off our knees as if we were learning to ride a bike. However, the good news is that as we mature in our faith, we go from glory to glory or victory to victory.

Day 302

What can you pray for today? God's will to be done in your life, in your family, in your church, in your city, in your nation, in the whole world (Matthew 6:10). Provision personal and family needs to be met (Matthew 6:11). Forgiveness receive forgiveness from God and forgive those who have offended you (Matthew 6:12). Victory over temptation and protection from the devil's schemes (Matthew 6:13).

Day 303

You have to set your will to forgive or your prayer time is wasted! "In prayer, there is a connection between what God does and what you do. You can't get forgiveness from God, for instance, without also forgiving others" (Matthew 6:14, MSG).

Day 304

I have friends that I love in various religions. Sometimes it's hard to tell them about Jesus because you don't want to offend them or jeopardize the friendship or business relationship. That's cool because your Christ-like life, decisions, and actions will speak. Then the Holy Spirit will provide you an opportunity to tell them about your relationship with Jesus! Let's go! (John 14:6, MSG).

Day 305

Do you have enemies trying to get you fired, destroy your marriage, come against your children, or mess up your business? Be encouraged, the Bible says: "Plan and plot all you want—nothing will come of it. All your talk is mere talk, empty words, because when all is said and done, the last word is Immanuel—God-With-Us. A boulder blocking your way (Isaiah 8:10, MSG).

Day 306

We need unity in God for more peace in the world! (Luke 11:17, MSG).

Day 307

Real religion, the kind that passes muster before God the Father, is this: Reach out to the homeless and loveless in their plight, and guard against corruption from the godless world. The Royal Rule of Love" (James 1:27, MSG).

Day 308

The Bible says, "The wealth of the wicked is stored up for the righteous?" I believe there will be wealth transference before the return of Christ! Are you eligible?

Day 309

You can't change until your mind has changed! Willpower is only a temporary fix! "And be not fashioned according to this world: but be ye transformed by the renewing of your mind, and ye may prove what is the good and acceptable and perfect will of God" (Romans 12:2, ASV).

Day 310

Do you want to be truly successful? "Study this book of instruction continually. Meditate on it day and night so you will be sure to obey everything written in it. Only then will you prosper and succeed in all you do." Let's go together! (Joshua 1:8, NLT).

Day 311

How can I resist temptation? Jesus resisted temptation, not by willpower, but by knowing and quoting God's Word. We can win the temptation war the same way, by knowing and speaking God's Word (Matthew 4:3–4).

Day 312

Head knowledge and religious facts don't produce purity and holiness. The Word planted deep in our hearts will keep us away from sin (Psalms 119:9, 11).

Day 313

"Like newborn babies, you must crave pure spiritual milk so that you will grow into a full experience of salvation. Cry out for this nourishment." Some Christians never experience the fullness of God after salvation. They become a minimum-wage Christian (just enough to get by and can't help anybody else)! God wants you to be a CEO Christian to employ and help others! (1 Peter 2:2, NLT).

Day 314

"Too much talk leads to sin. Be sensible and keep your mouth shut" (Proverbs 10:19, NLT).

Day 315

Some of us are given godly gifts such as speaking in tongues or a heavenly language. However, this must be done in decency and in order. "So anyone who speaks in tongues should pray also for the ability to interpret what has been said" (1 Corinthians 14:13, NLT).

Day 316

The first time I heard someone speaking in tongues, it scared the daylights out of me. I had no idea what they were saying! "A person who speaks in tongues is strengthened personally, but one who speaks a word of prophecy strengthens the entire church" (1 Corinthians 14:4, NLT).

Day 317

"For if you have the ability to speak in tongues, you will be talking only to God, since people won't be able to understand you. You will be speaking by the power of the Spirit, but it will all be mysterious." Father, thank You for this gift—another level in You by your grace and mercy! If you ask God and believe, then this gift is available to you as well!

Day 318

Today let love be your highest goal! Everyone has one family member who gets on your nerves every Thanksgiving! That is a perfect opportunity to put those spiritual muscles to work! Surprise them with kindness and check out their response!

Day 319

Do you want to see real change in the USA? Then pray and vote for godly men and women to be in position of government—not a political party! "When the godly are in authority, the people rejoice. But when the wicked are in power, they groan" (Proverbs 29:2, NLT).

Day 320

I wonder how many women in today's society are willing to submit to a godly husband. We don't see much of that emulated on television.

Day 321

Alert: Jesus is coming back! "Men of Galilee," they said, "why are you standing here staring into heaven? Jesus has been taken from you into heaven, but someday he will return from heaven in the same way you saw him go!" (Acts 1:11, NLT).

Day 322

"A good woman is hard to find, and worth far more than diamonds. Her husband trusts her without reserve, and never has reason to regret it. Never spiteful, she treats him generously all her life long. She looks over a field and buys it, then, with money she's put aside, plants a garden."

—The Bible (Men, sorry, but you usually will not find these on the set at the video shoot or in the club!)

Day 323

To all those in leadership and authority (political, social, economical) we have a responsibility to God who put us in those positions! "Speak up for the people who have no voice, for the rights of all the down-and-outers. Speak out for justice! Stand up for the poor and destitute!" (Proverbs 31:8–9).

Day 324

Jesus's last words before going to heaven were to instruct us to tell others about him! "But you will receive power when the Holy Spirit comes upon you. And you will be my witnesses, telling people about me everywhere—in Jerusalem, throughout Judea, in Samaria, and to the ends of the earth." We most open our mouths to tell someone about Jesus daily! (Acts 1:8, NLT).

Day 325

God loves you from the uttermost to the guttermost! You can't even imagine—it's like an ant doing a root canal!

Day 326

So what should you do when you are being tempted and feel like giving in and giving up? Refuse! Just keep your focus on the Lord and rejoice in His faithfulness. Remember that God is not a man so He cannot lie. He will see you through!

Day 327

"The temptations in your life are no different from what others experience. And God is faithful. He will not allow the temptation to be more than you can stand. When you are tempted, he will show you a way out so that you can endure." You can't beat being a Christian with a hammer. Thank you Lord! (1 Corinthians 10:13, NLT).

Day 328

When Satan attacks us, we must remember that God is in control. God has given us great promises. Jesus saves. Jesus keeps. His salvation is eternal. He didn't bring us this far to leave us. He didn't teach us to swim to let us drown. He didn't build His home in us to move away. He didn't lift us up to let us down. You are more than a conqueror in Christ and will make it!

Day 329

Following Christ is a matter of the will and the mind, not of feelings alone. Feelings are like the wind (can change directions at any time). Faith in Christ is our solid anchor regardless of any storm. Give Him the opportunity to show up and show out in your situation by trusting Him today! He enjoys doing that for His children!

Day 330

Don't ask God to enlarge your territory until you become responsible for what you've already got. Do you keep it clean, share it with others, are you thankful for it, willing to give it away if God told you? The stuff!

Day 331

Every Christian has had a season of rebellion before coming to the Lord! Don't let them fool you! In fact, some of the most inspiring preachers are the ones who've done the most dirt! God loves using that kind to display his power, mercy, and grace! He is interested in using your dirt to build His kingdom!

Day 332

Lord, if I'm only able to help just one person on this earth, then I know my living was not in vain.

Day 333

Discouragement: Satan wants you to think that you can't change, and that it is impossible for you to let go of old mind-sets and habits. Don't believe him for a minute! Put your confidence in God and His Word. Believe what He has said about you, and know that when the knowledge of God's Word is on the inside of you, you will be equipped to make decisions that keep you on the path to change.

—Creflo Dollar

Day 334

Good things fall apart so that better things can fall in place! Good is the enemy of better and best! Never be complacent with good—always strive for better. You will never get more than you are willing to settle for! Even when you don't understand what's going on, God has a better plan for you! He is able and willing to do exceedingly more than you can ask or even think!

—Bishop Dale C. Bronner

Day 335

In life, we are like an empty bottle floating in the ocean (God). One day, we let God in and He fills all of the empty space. We then sink into his ways. We can never understand all of His ways just as we can never get the whole ocean into the bottle!

Day 336

Someone needs to move forward now in the things of God! How? (1) Accept what can't be changed, (2) give it up to God and leave it, and (3) focus on what is left, not lost.

Day 337

Know Jesus = know truth! No Jesus = no truth! Do you know or do you no ... Him?

Day 338

Christ is the source of every right impulse. He is the only one that can implant in the heart enmity (hatred) against sin. You can't do it by willpower or watching your favorite talk show host! Ask him today to reveal and work out the things in your life that are not like him. Be patient it's for your own good!

Day 339

Just because I wrote this book does not mean I am perfect! I don't have it all together yet! I am learning from my mistakes. Forgetting those things behind and pressing toward the mark of the high calling!

Day 340

Did you wake up with pain or worries this morning? Don't allow the enemy to talk you out of your position in Christ. He will attempt to discourage you by saying that you will never be healed, nor become an overcomer. That's one of Satan's favorite tricks! He knows your potential for bringing light into this dark world. Recite: I am more than a conqueror through Christ and will fulfill the will of God for my life!

Day 341

"Make allowance for each other's faults, and forgive anyone who offends you. Remember, the Lord forgave you, so you must forgive others" (Colossians 3:13, NLT).

Day 342

It's good to see people encouraging one another! That's how we Christians do it! Let the light shine so other can see us—not just in word, but also in deed. Have *Joy* prioritized:
J—Jesus
O—Others
Y—Yourself
—Pastor Jason Bolin

Day 343

These are some common reasons that people doubt salvation: (1) People want to feel something. (2) People are struggling with certain sins. (3) People have received bad teaching. (4) People want to contribute something.

Day 344

How do you know if you are saved? Here are some signs: (1) You have remorse for sin and desire holiness. (2) You will grow in love for people. (3) You will have an inward witness. (4) You trust Jesus alone for your salvation. (5) Your righteousness is by faith and not works.

Day 345

Confessing Jesus is Lord implies a submission to His Lordship in every area of life. This is easier said than done. This will take practice and a conscious effort. If Jesus is not Lord of all, He's not Lord at all. Help us, Lord, to understand and apply this principle daily.

Day 346

Most people are ignorant because they don't like to read! God says my people are destroyed due to lack of knowledge! Someone said that if you want to hide something, just put it in a Bible!

Day 347

If you confess with your mouth that Jesus is Lord and believe in your heart that God raised Him from the dead, you will be saved" (Romans 10:9, NLT).

Day 348
If you refresh others, you too will be refreshed!

Day 349
For Christ himself has brought peace to us. He united Jews and Gentiles into one people when, in His own body on the cross, He broke down the wall of hostility that separated us." Think about that! (Ephesians 2:14, NLT).

Day 350

We need to get the *church* out of the church and out into the *streets*!

Day 351

Think about this! Would you be upset if you gave someone your most precious item (such as your child) that you love and adore then they turned around and stomped on it (him or her)! Well, that's how God feels when we reject Jesus, His only son!

Day 352

God gave the promises to Abraham and his child. And notice that the Scripture doesn't say "to his children," as if it meant many descendants. Rather, it says "to his child." That, of course, means Christ. We are joint heirs to the promise as a Christian by faith! The good news is that this opportunity is available to anyone (race, gender, rich, or poor)! (Galatians 3:16, NLT).

Day 353

There is a new level of peace and joy when you meditate (read and ponder) God's Word in the morning and at night. You should try it today and see what happens!

Day 354

Statistics in 2010: 72 percent of black children are born to single mothers. 63 percent of youth suicides are from fatherless homes; 90 percent of homeless and runaway children are from fatherless homes; 85 percent of children with behavior disorders are from fatherless homes; 80 percent of rapists with anger problems are from fatherless homes; 71 percent of high school dropouts are from fatherless homes; 75 percent of kids in drug centers are from fatherless homes; and 85 percent of youth in prison are from fatherless homes! We need Jesus!

Day 355

Did you know that God has a plan? "And this is God's plan: Both Gentiles and Jews who believe the Good News share equally in the riches inherited by God's children. Both are part of the same body, and both enjoy the promise of blessings because they belong to Christ Jesus." A Gentile is someone who is not a Jew (Ephesians 3:6, NLT).

Day 356

When your memories exceed your dreams, your end is near.
—Pastor Jason Bolin

Day 357

"The eye can never say to the hand, 'I don't need you.' The head can't say to the feet, 'I don't need you.'" We really need each other to walk in victory as Christians! (1 Corinthians 12:21, NLT).

Day 358

Sometimes you may wonder why you were born a certain way, in a certain family, or have certain bad habits (addictions)—especially after being a born-again Christian. Relax! Pray sincerely to God, change what you can, and let Him do the rest. The problem comes when we want instant change or success. He does not work like that most of the time. It's a process! The world was not created in one day and surely He had the power to do it, but decided to methodically and purposely put it together in a process. That's how He works on us! This will strengthen you and allow you to stand once delivered! We all have a separate part to play—just like our body parts! In order to have a functional body, many parts must come together in unison—hence the "body of Christ."

Day 359

I look forward to paying my bills! Why? Because when someone owes me money, I look forward to them paying me. The Golden Rule works!

Day 360

We are always in a battle on earth—maybe not physically, but spiritually. As long as Satan is still roaming the earth, he has you on his target. We must put on the full armor of God—not only for protection, but for aggression. We must use the spirit of truth (words) as our sword. We must pursue the enemy (expose him)! Hunt him down and make him pay us seven times what he stole from us!

Day 361

Some of us can't *stand* for God long because we never *sat* with him long enough!

—Pastor Jason Bolin

Day 362

Have you ever been upset because you didn't win the lottery? God has a better plan for you! See it is one thing to be rich in this world, but it is another to be rich for eternity! God's Word will provide you the combination for both. Remember that being rich is a very subjective word. A millionaire with terminal cancer is broke! Think about that! Let's go!

Day 363

Don't let godless people who get rich discourage you! If it's not gained honestly, then it won't last. Think of Bernie Madoff's Ponzi scheme! "Evil people get rich for the moment, but the reward of the godly will last" (Proverbs 11:18, NLT).

Day 364

"People ruin their own lives and then blame it on God" (Proverbs 19:3).

Day 365

I'd rather fail with honor than succeed by fraud.

—Sophocles

About the Author

Dr. Rico Short is known as Endodontist or Root Canal Specialist to the Stars! He has treated numerous celebrities from actors, producers, writers, comedians, television anchors, sport athletes, and music artists. Dr. Short has also been featured in several publications, radio and television shows, internet blogs, and journals. He has attained countless awards and recognition in the area of dentistry and motivational speaking. In addition, Dr. Short serves as an expert Board Certified Root Canal Consultant to the Georgia Board of Dentistry. He is also an associate clinical professor at the Medical College of Georgia School of Dentistry. His practice (Apex Endodontics P.C) is located in Smyrna, Georgia (www.apexendodontics.net).

Dr. Short has been a featured speaker to youth groups all over the country. His main focus is to encourage the youth to set goals and give them realistic advise on how to achieve them. Dr. Short's daily inspiration and motivation can be followed on facebook and twitter.

Dr. Rico Short was born in Columbus Georgia on June 29, 1974. He was reared from a single family household by a mother who worked 33 years on the floor in a textile mill. Growing up as a child, Dr. Short said he did not have a lot of "things" but he had a lot of love, prayer, and support from his family. Dr. Short said his mother had to "drag" him to church because he really did not see the importance as a teenager. However, now as an adult, his Christian foundation has become the bedrock for all of his success.

Dr. Short is married to Angela Short who is a dental hygienist by profession. They have two children: Jayla and Ava. Dr. Short attributes his accomplishments to an understanding and loving wife and kids but most of all to his Lord and Savior Jesus Christ.